COUNT with Me

counting with

SUPERHEROES

by John Wood

Gareth Stevens
PUBLISHING

Please visit our website, www.garethstevens.com.
For a free color catalog of all our high-quality books,
call toll free 1-800-542-2595 or fax 1-877-542-2596.

Cataloging-in-Publication Data

Names: Wood, John, author. | Li, Amy, illustrator.
Title: Counting with superheroes / by John Wood, illustrated by Amy Li.
Description: New York : Gareth Stevens, 2023. | Series: Count with me
Identifiers: ISBN 9781538281826 (pbk.) | ISBN 9781538281840 (library
bound) | ISBN 9781538281833 (6 pack) | ISBN 9781538281857 (ebook)
Subjects: LCSH: Counting--Juvenile literature. | Superheroes--Juvenile
literature.
Classification: LCC QA113.W66 2023 | DDC 513.2'11--dc23

Published in 2023 by
Gareth Stevens Publishing
29 East 21st Sreet
New York, NY 10010

Edited by:
Madeline Tyler

Illustrated by:
Amy Li

Printed in the United States of America

CPSIA compliance information: Batch #CSGS23: For further information contact Gareth Stevens,
New York, New York at 1-800-542-2595.

Find us on

Photo Credits

Images are courtesy of Shutterstock.com. With thanks to Getty
Images, Thinkstock Photo and iStockphoto.

Recurring images – vectoring (comic bubbles), studiostoks
(background pattern), vector Tradition (number pattern),
WinWin a rtlab (fire hero symbol), Dantetaia (strong hero
symbol), Nebur (ice hero symbol), Mental Hart (smart hero
symbol). Cover – p1 – Art998, Owens Graphic Studio. p12–13
– nienjaze, Pop and hot, PiXXart. p16–17 – glmark. p22–23 –
Andrew Rybalko, Malysam Droizd. p24 – WinWin arttab.

The people in this building need help.

We need to save them from...

1 big volcano!

Freeze the lava!

Well done.

Up we go!

We need to save someone from...

5

We must go to the next floor.

We need to save someone from...

3 scary snowmen!

Melt the snow!

8

9

4 giant robots!

POW!

They were built to be good,
but they have gone wrong.

We need to
keep going.

We need to save someone from....

But we need to save someone else from...

That has scared them off.

Now we need to save someone from...

8 trapdoors!

That is a long way to fall.

Make them float!

Well done.

But now we need to save someone from...

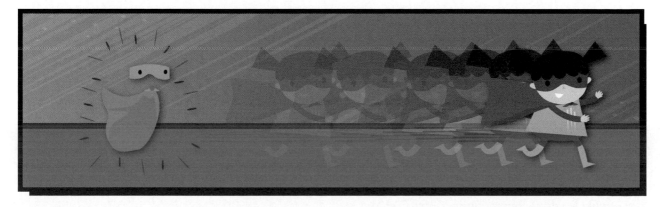

9 evil cameras!

Press the button
to turn them off,
but do not be seen!

She must go to the top of the building.

She needs to save someone from...

10 thunderclouds!

Crash!

That child should not be out here in a storm.

Zigzag around the lightning and grab the child!